TAO TE CHING
ILLUSTRATED

THE WAY TO GOODNESS AND POWER

LAO TZU

amber
BOOKS

This Amber illustrated edition first published in 2023

Reprinted in 2024

Amber Books Ltd
United House
North Road
London N7 9DP
United Kingdom
www.amberbooks.co.uk
Facebook: amberbooks
YouTube: amberbooksltd
Instagram: amberbooksltd
X(Twitter): @amberbooks

Copyright © 2017 Amber Books Ltd

All rights reserved. No part of this work may be reproduced,
stored in a retrieval system, or transmitted in any form or by
any means, electronic, mechanical, photocopying, recording,
or otherwise, without the prior permission of the copyright holder.

ISBN: 978-1-83886-273-2

Translator: James Trapp

Printed and bound in China

James Trapp took his degree in Chinese at SOAS, University of London, specializing in Bronze Age art and archaeology and early Buddhist sculpture. Until recently he was the China Education Manager at the British Museum and currently works at the Confucius Institute at the Institute of Education, University of London, promoting and supporting the study of Chinese in English schools.

PICTURE CREDITS
Alamy: 3 (Heritage Images) 21 (Valerii Shanin), 25 & 32 (Print Collector), 38 (Interfoto), 41 (Maximages),
    43 (Interfoto), 67 (Print Collector), 70 (David Lyons), 77 (Victor Paul Borg), 81 (Interfoto), 84 (Well/BOT),
    96 (Ivy Close Studios), 118 (Image Professionals)
Alamy/CPA Media: 8, 11, 15, 60, 78, 88, 99, 116, 128, 132, 148
Cleveland Museum of Art: 156
Getty Images: 36 (Heritage Images), 74 (Universal Images Group), 90 (Roger Viollet Collection),
    111 (Burstein Collection), 120 (Heritage Images), 126 (De Agostini), 131 (Heritage Images), 135 (De Agostini),
    140 (Indianapolis Museum of Art at Newfields)
LA County Museum of Art: 100
Metropolitan Museum of Art, New York: 12, 17, 18, 26, 29, 35, 44, 48, 51, 55, 56, 59, 63, 64, 68, 73, 87,
    93, 104, 107, 108, 113, 115, 123, 136, 139, 143, 144, 147, 151, 153
Museum of Asian Art/Smithsonian: 22, 159
Public Domain: 47
Walters Art Museum: 103

TRADITIONAL CHINESE BOOKBINDING
This book has been produced using traditional Chinese bookbinding techniques, using a method that was developed during the Ming Dynasty (1368–1644) and remained in use until the adoption of Western binding techniques in the early 1900s. In traditional Chinese binding, single sheets of paper are printed on one side only, and each sheet is folded in half, with the printed pages on the outside. The book block is then sandwiched between two boards and sewn together through punched holes close to the cut edges of the folded sheets.

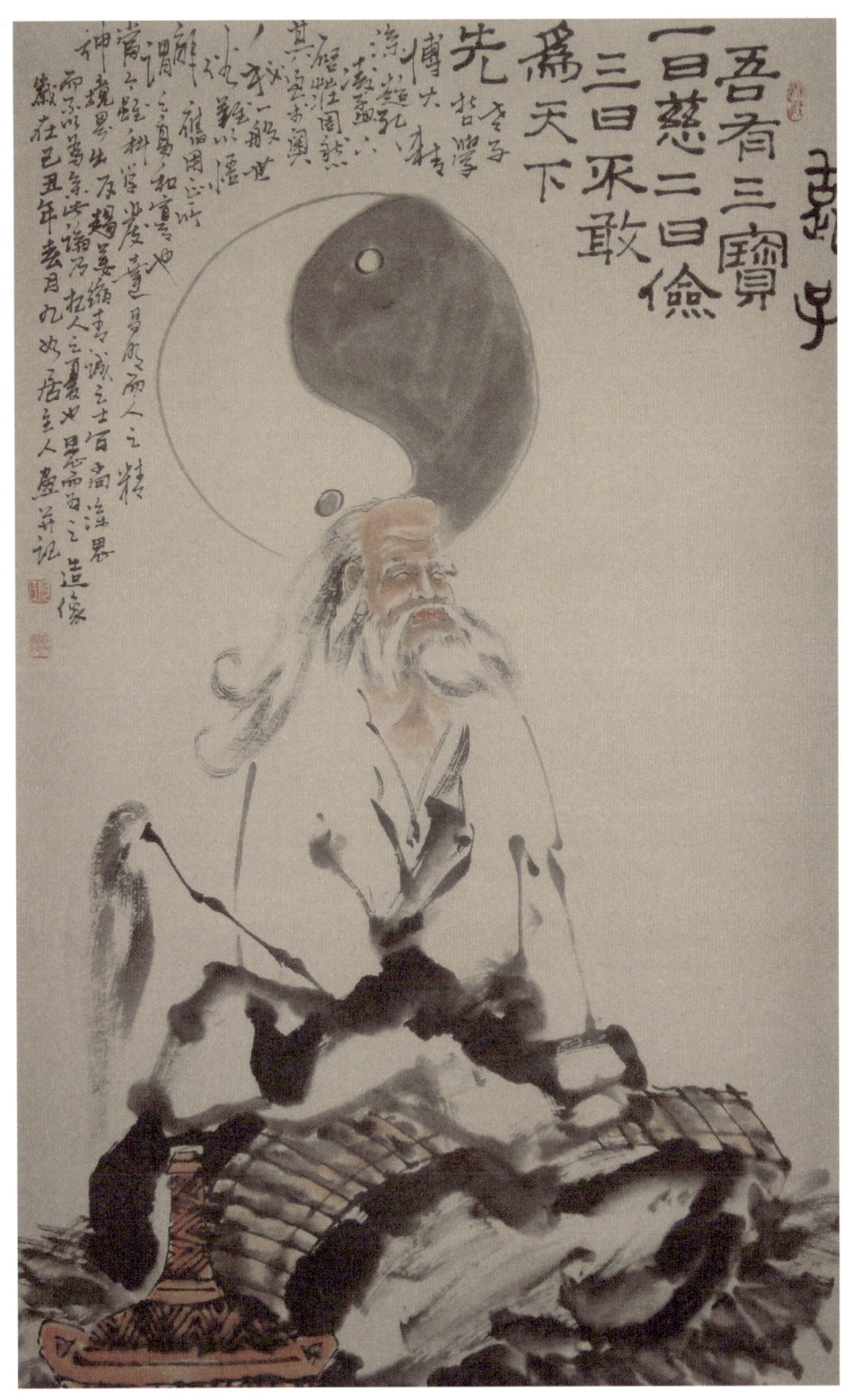

A depiction of 'Lao Tzu' – author of the Daodejing (Tao Te Ching)

Introduction

Daodejing (道德經) probably holds the record for the most variants in translation of any work of literature, and this new version can make no more claim to 'accuracy' than any other. Its aim is to offer a degree of clarity and coherence that is sometimes missing. This is not a snide criticism of other translators, but an acknowledgement that for the purposes of this book certain definite decisions were taken about the nature of the original text. They are no more right or wrong than many others. That is part and parcel of the enigma of this extraordinary work.

Old Master

According to tradition, Daodejing was written by a single author, known as Laozi (老子) around the 6th century BC. Laozi, in fact, is an honorific title, translating as Old Master, rather than an actual name. If he actually existed, his personal name is generally given as Li Er (李耳), with the posthumous name Li Dan (李聃). He is so described in the Shiji (史記) the Records of the Grand Historian of China written by Sima Qian (司馬遷) in the late 2nd century BCE. In fact, just as with Homer in Greek literature, it is unlikely that there ever was such a person, and the work is an accumulation of a variety of sources. There are a number of different source texts, both partial and complete, with the earliest, discovered on bamboo slips excavated in 1993 near Guodian in Hubei Province, dating from some time around 300 BC, in the Warring States Period. The other significant early original text also came from archaeological excavations in neighbouring Hunan Province, at the extraordinary site at Mawangdui, and is written on miraculously preserved silk. It dates to 2nd century BCE in the Western Han Dynasty. The other principle texts are from commentaries written by scholars in the first three centuries CE in the Eastern Han Dynasty and Three Kingdoms Period. This translation has essentially followed the text of one of the three later commentaries, that of Wang Bi (王弼, 226-249 CE), with a small number of emendations from other versions where sense and context seemed to make them preferable. These changes only ever alter nuance rather than fundamental meaning.

The standard modern text of Daodejing comprises around 5000 characters divided into 81 chapters. It also divides into two parts, the Daojing, Classic of the Dao (1-37), and the Dejing, the Classic of Virtue (38-81). There is no certainty that this was their original order, and the division of the chapters

may also be a later formulation. Whatever its antecedents, however, the work is, and has long been, firmly established as Daodejing, the Classic of the Way and of Virtue.

Interpreting Daodejing

There are many different ways of interpreting Daodejing. In terms of language, all ancient classical Chinese is highly elliptical and the Daodejing exceptionally so, spare even in its use of the marker particles that give a syntactical framework. In addition there are frequent references to things that may have been common knowledge in the Warring States Period but whose precise meaning and symbolism are long lost. For the most part these barriers are negotiable, but in crossing them the translator and reader face the real challenge of interpretation: what is the underlying nature of the book? For some it is a mythological and mystic work with roots deep in ancient tradition, and representing the remains of an ancient cosmology. It is seen as the sacred text of the religious beliefs that came to be known as Daoism. For others, the religious aspect is entirely secondary and it is taken as a work of metaphysical philosophy rooted more in practicality than mysticism. Finally, and this is the view taken for this translation, it can be seen as a work of socio-political philosophy possibly written specifically as guidance for the ruler of a small to medium-sized state. The text contains specific instructions and admonitions to such a ruler, which are dictated by and dependent on the over-arching mystic cosmology. In this translation, the deliberately opaque or unfathomably mysterious possibilities the text offers have, in general, given place to an attempt at clarity and consistency within the constraints of the text itself and its assumed purpose. At the same time, no translation of this work can allow itself to cast aside the essential lyricism and unfettered embracing of paradox of the original. The sole purpose here is to offer another avenue for readers to explore this extraordinary work for themselves.

The Bagua *are eight trigrams used in Daoist cosmology to represent the fundamental principles of reality. The template for each has eight areas arranged in an octogram shape. At the centre are the characters for yin and yang.*

CHAPTER 1

The Mystery of the Dao[1]

道可道，非常道。名可名，非常名。無名天地之始；有名萬物之母。故常無欲，以觀其妙；常有欲，以觀其徼。此兩者，同出而異名，同謂之玄。玄之又玄，眾妙之門。

The Dao that we can comprehend is not the eternal and infinite Dao
The names that we give are not the eternal and infinite names
Void is how we name the origin of the Cosmos
Amplitude is how we name the creation of the things that fill it
Thus it is in Void that we can contemplate the scope of the Dao
And in Amplitude, its subtleties.
These two have different names but a common source
And both are mysteries.
They are mystery upon mystery,
Gateways to the infinite mutability of the Dao.

---

[1] The Chinese word 道 is in common current use meaning a road, a way or a path in both concrete and figurative senses. But in this context, as the following 81 chapters will make clear, it embodies much more than this, and defies translation. Indeed it could be said that it has no specific meaning, or at least means infinitely more than a word or phrase can encompass. I have chosen to stay with the pinyin romanization 'Dao' and leave the reader to interpret it.

CHAPTER 2

Not-doing

天下皆知美之為美，斯惡已。皆知善之為善，斯不善已。故有無相生，難易相成，長短相較，高下相傾，音聲相和，前後相隨。恒也。是以聖人處無為之事，行不言之教；萬物作而弗始，生而不有。為而不恃，功成而弗居。夫唯弗居，是以不去。

If we understand what makes Beauty beautiful, then we can recognize Ugliness
If we understand what makes Goodness good, then we can recognize the Bad
Void and Amplitude have the same origin
Difficulty and Ease beget each other
Long and Short define each other
High and Low support each other
Music and Voice harmonize with each other
Before and After follow each other
This is the Constant.
From this it follows that the wise man acts through Not-doing,
Teaches without words
And interacts with Creation without initiating.
He makes but does not own,
Acts but does not rely on the result,
Achieves but does not linger to be recognized.
In not seeking recognition, his credit becomes enduring.

This hanging scroll painting shows Nanji Changsheng Dadi, the 'Great Emperor of Longevity of the South Pole', third of the Four Heavenly Ministers (Siyu) of Daoism.

Leaning on a staff for support, a gentleman pauses on a mountain path to gaze into a misty void (ink on paper, 1660s).

CHAPTER 3

Removing Desire

不尚賢, 使民不爭; 不貴難得之貨, 使民不為盜; 不見可欲, 使心不亂。是以聖人之治, 虛其心, 實其腹, 弱其志, 強其骨。常使民無知無欲。使夫知者不敢為也。為無為, 則無不治。

If talent is not glorified, people will not compete with one another

If the rare and precious are not coveted, people will not steal

If desirable objects are not wantonly displayed, people's hearts will not be in turmoil

When the enlightened man orders things he bestows a mind empty of needless concerns; a stomach full of nourishing food. He eschews selfish resolve, and strengthens the body

As a guiding principle he removes the opportunities for wilfulness and covetousness from the ordinary people, and withholds the opportunities for misusing their knowledge from the educated.

In doing by Not-doing, there is nothing that cannot be controlled.

CHAPTER 4

The Infinite Dao

道沖而用之或不盈。淵兮似萬物之宗。挫其銳, 解其紛, 和其光, 同其塵。湛兮似或存。吾不知誰之子, 象帝之先。

The Dao is like a bowl that can never be emptied

Truly it is inexhaustible, the fount of Creation

It blunts the sharp

Resolves the tangled

Softens the dazzling

Settles the dust cloud

Truly it is unfathomable, and yet we know it is there

I do not know what gave birth to the Dao, but surely it precedes the Sage Emperors[2].

---

[2] In Chinese mythology and traditional chronology, the 3rd millennium BC saw the time of the three Sovereigns and five Emperors (三皇五帝). The three Sovereigns were divine creators, and the five Emperors human rulers of exemplary morality and wisdom.

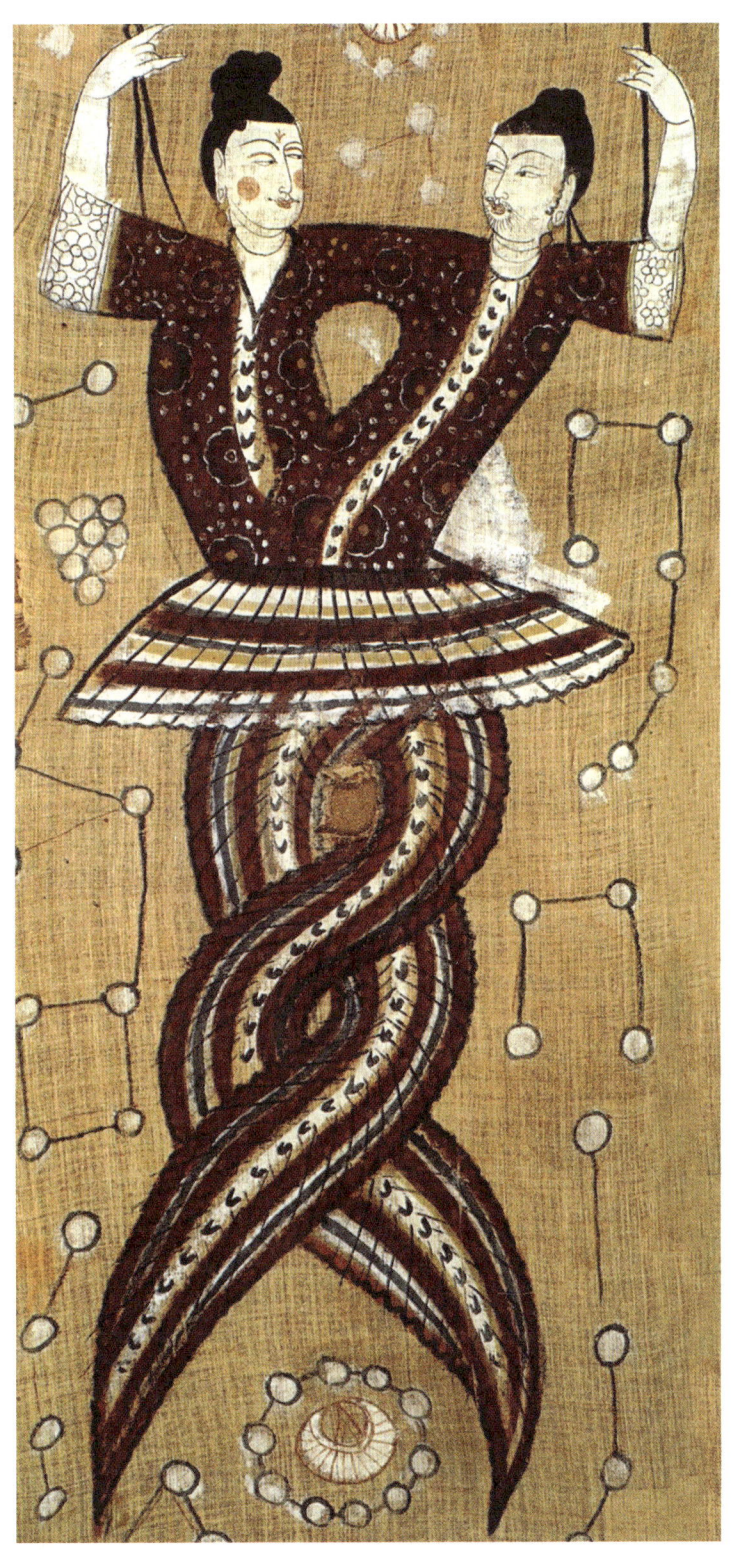

The creator divinities Fuxi (right) and Nuwa (left) intertwined. Hanging scroll painting, 8th century.

CHAPTER 5

Cultivating Emptiness

天地不仁，以萬物為芻狗；聖人不仁，以百姓為芻狗。天地之間，其猶橐籥乎？虛而不屈，動而愈出。多言數窮，不如守中。

The Cosmos obeys its own rules and has no inclination to benevolence

It treats Creation like ritual objects to be used according to their purpose

The Wise Man obeys his own rules and has no natural inclination to benevolence

He treats the people like ritual objects to be used according to their purpose

Is the Cosmos not like a pair of bellows?

Bellows are empty but inexhaustible and the more they are worked the more they produce

The more we try to define, the more we diminish; far better to cherish unspoken inner understanding.

Fang Congyi, a 14th century Daoist priest from Jiangxi, traveled extensively in the north before settling down at the Shangqing Temple on Mount Longhu (Dragon Tiger Mountain), Jiangxi province. In 'Cloudy Mountains', the painter's kinetic brushwork, wound up as if in a whirlwind, charges the mountains with an expressive liveliness that defies their physical structure. The great mountain range, weightless and dematerialized, resembles a dragon ascending into the clouds.

'Landscapes in Summer and Winter', by Ike Taiga (18th century).

CHAPTER 6

The Spirit of the Valley[3]

谷神不死,是謂玄牝。玄牝之門,是謂天地根。綿綿若存,用之不勤。

The Spirit of the Valley is the sacred feminine principle
Its gateway is the root of the Cosmos
Like an unbroken silk thread, it is inexhaustible.

CHAPTER 7

Self Through Selflessness

天長地久。天地所以能長且久者,以其不自生故能長生。是以聖人後其身而身先;外其身而身存。以其無私,故能成其私。

Heaven is long-lasting and Earth is enduring.
Thus, as it is in itself long-lasting and enduring but does not exist for its own benefit
The Cosmos may endure
In the same way the enlightened man may place himself last but come first
And may neglect himself and yet be preserved.
It is his lack of self-interest that allows him to fulfil his self.

---

[3] The valley is a recurring image throughout the text. It represents the power of the yin in that it is dark, wet, empty yet carries the intense potential of fertility, and is a conduit for the life force. The nature of the yin/feminine is most clearly articulated in Chapter 61: "The female eternally subdues the male through passivity/In passivity it is receptive" and its potential in Chapter 28: "The man who understands his masculine nature/But also cherishes the feminine/ Is like a mountain stream for the world".

CHAPTER 8

Avoiding Conflict

上善若水。水善利萬物而不爭,處眾人之所惡,故幾於道。居善地,心善淵,與善仁,言善信,正善治,事善能,動善時。夫唯不爭,故無尤。

People of the highest virtue are like water

Water benefits Creation without any conflict

And it favours the low places shunned by the common people

In this it resembles the Dao

Live in harmony with the land

Allow emotions to run deep

Show benevolence in your dealings with others

Speak with honesty

Arrange things according to the proper order

Manage according to your ability

Act according to opportunity

Without conflict, there is no animosity.

Two Daoist gods sit on a rock in heaven (Chengdu, China).

'Ge Hong Moving House', Ming dynasty, 16th century.

CHAPTER 9

Recognizing Sufficiency

持而盈之，不如其已；揣而銳之，不可長保。金玉滿堂，莫之能守；富貴而驕，自遺其咎。功成身退天之道。

If a vessel you are carrying is already full
It is best not to add anything more
If you keep trying the edge of a blade
You will blunt it
Halls full of gold and jade are impossible to safeguard
Pride in wealth and honour brings its own downfall
To retire gracefully once your task is done
That is the way of the Dao.

CHAPTER 10

Potential of the Dao

載營魄抱一能無離乎？專氣致柔能如嬰兒乎？滌除玄覽能無疵乎？愛民治國能無為乎？天門開闔能為雌乎？明白四達能無知乎？生之、畜之，生而不有為而不恃長而不宰是謂玄德。

When the *hun* and the *po*[4] conform to the Dao
Are they not inseparable?
When you concentrate *qi*[5] to its utmost suppleness
Can you not return to the state of a new-born child?
If you wash away dark thoughts
Can you not render yourself flawless?
 If love of the common people directs your government of the state
Can you not rule through Not-doing?
As the gates of Heaven open and close in the cycle of life
Can you not adhere to the female principle?
Through understanding the whole scope of the Four Directions
Can you not act without intent?
To create and nurture but not claim ownership
To act but not glory in the action
To guide but not control
This is the deep virtue of the Dao.

---

[4] At around the time the Daodejing was traditionally being written, a new development in belief about the human soul and the after-life was developing. Before that time, humans were believed only to have one soul, essentially the *po* (魄), but with the development of Daoist concepts of the duality of *yin* (陰) and *yang* (陽), came the idea of two types of soul: the *po* which is *yin*, and the *hun* (魂) which is yang. The *hun* is the aethereal, spiritual soul which ascends to the heavens after death, and the po is a corporeal, substantive soul which remains on earth in the parallel after-life the deceased now inhabits.

[5] *Qi* (氣) is the life-force that permeates all of creation. In humans it is drawn in from the air through the top of the head, and from the ground through the feet. It circulates through the body sustaining life, health and energy. Regulating its smooth flow along the body's meridians is the basis of acupuncture, and this, along with keeping the complimenting energies of *yin* and *yang* in balance, are the fundamentals of Traditional Chinese Medicine. All of the important ancient philosophers, Confucius, Zhuangzi, Laozi, Mozi and others make reference to the importance of *qi*.

Nu Gua, the mother goddess of Chinese mythology, had a human head and the body of a snake. She was the creator of humankind and matchmaker credited with inventing the idea of marriage.

Wheel of the Buddhist Law (Rinpō) (late 13th century).

CHAPTER 11

The Power of the Insubstantial

三十輻共一轂 當其無，有車之用。埏埴以為器 當其無，有器之用。鑿戶牖以為室 當其無，有室之用。故有之以為利，無之以為用。

Thirty spokes meet in the hub of a wheel
But it is the empty space at the centre that makes it useful for a cart
Clay is used to make a pot
But it is the empty space within that makes it useful as a container
Windows and doors pierce the walls of a room
But it is the space within that makes it useful as a dwelling
Thus things with substance are practical
But it is the insubstantial that is productive.

CHAPTER 12

Subjugation of Desire

五色令人目盲；五音令人耳聾；五味令人口爽；馳騁田獵，令人心發狂；難得之貨，令人行妨。是以聖人為腹不為目，故去彼取此。

Too many colours confuse the eye

Too many sounds confuse the ear

Too many tastes confuse the palate

A life of hectic pleasure, riding and hunting will drive you crazy

Coveting precious objects destroys your morals.

The wise man is concerned only with having a full belly, not with vain aspirations

He concentrates on the former and distances himself from the latter.

'Daoist Immortals in a Landscape' (16th century). This painting invites the viewer to follow a mountain path across a stone arch and into a magical realm where herb gatherers dressed in garments of leaves and grass mingle with robed gentlemen engaged in scholarly pleasures: viewing paintings, playing weiqi, *strumming a zither, composing poetry, engaging in 'pure conversation', and contemplating the scenery.*

CHAPTER 13

Avoidance of Danger

寵辱若驚，貴大患若身。何謂寵辱若驚？寵為上，辱為下，得之若驚，失之若驚，是謂寵辱若驚。何謂貴大患若身？吾所以有大患者，為吾有身，及吾無身，吾有何患？故貴以身為天下，則可寄天下；愛以身為天下，乃可託天下。

Favour and disgrace are equally perilous
And each should be given the same respect as your own life.
Why do I say favour and disgrace are equally perilous?
Favour raises you to the heights
Disgrace plunges you to the depths
Both situations are equally perilous.
Why do I say they should be given the same respect as your own life?
If you encounter great peril, it is so because it threatens your life.
If you do not have life, what peril can threaten you?
Thus a person who holds his life in greater respect than the whole kingdom
Is fit to be entrusted with the kingdom.
A person who loves his life more than the whole kingdom
Is fit to be entrusted with the kingdom.

CHAPTER 14

The Essence of the Dao

視之不見，名曰夷；聽之不聞，名曰希；搏之不得，名曰微。此三者不可致詰，故混而為一。其上不皦，其下不昧。繩繩不可名，復歸於無物。是謂無狀之狀，無物之象，是謂惚恍。迎之不見其首，隨之不見其後。執古之道，以御今之有。能知古始，是謂道紀。

To look but not to see is called *yi*

To listen but not to hear is called *xi*

To strive for but not to attain is called *wei* [6]

These three things are beyond our comprehension

Together they form the Dao

It is neither bright above nor dark below

Endlessly linked, it cannot be defined as it returns to nothingness –

The formless form

Shape without substance, it is called the Abstract

From in front you cannot see its beginning

From behind you cannot see its end.

Understand the ancient Dao to order the affairs of today.

This is the essence of the Dao.

---

[6] Even in modern Chinese there is no direct translation for these terms so they are best left as they stand with their own definitions.

'The Eight Immortals Crossing the Sea' (1922). The Eight Immortals are revered by Daoists and are a popular element of Chinese culture. They are said to live on a group of five islands in the Bohai Sea.

CHAPTER 15

Qualities of the Dao

古之善為士者，微妙玄通，深不可識。夫唯不可識，故強為之容。豫兮若冬涉川；猶兮若畏四鄰；儼兮其若容；渙兮若冰之將釋；敦兮其若樸；曠兮其若谷；混兮其若濁；濁以靜之徐清；安以動之徐生。保此道者，不欲盈。夫唯不盈，故能蔽不新成。

The adepts of old knew these mysteries in infinite detail

With profundity beyond our understanding

Since they are beyond our understanding, all we can do is strive to copy them

Cautious, so cautious – as though fording a river in winter

Circumspect, so circumspect – as though scanning every direction

Dignified, so dignified – like an honoured guest

Elusive, so elusive – like river ice melting

Straightforward like uncarved wood

Open like a broad valley

Confusing as a muddy river

Stillness will make the confusion clear

From stillness life can stir afresh and re-emerge

Those who follow the ancient Dao in this way do not seek completion

And because they do not seek completion, they can maintain themselves and do not need to be replaced.

CHAPTER 16

Returning to Origin

致虛極，守靜篤。萬物並作，吾以觀復。夫物芸芸，各復歸其根。歸根曰靜，靜曰復命。復命曰常，知常曰明。不知常，妄作凶。知常容，容乃公，公乃全，全乃天，天乃道，道乃久，沒身不殆。

Achieve a state of total emptiness, preserve a perfect stillness

The myriad elements of Creation rise and grow and I watch them repeat their endless cycle

Diverse and varied, everything returns to its origin

This return to origin is what we mean by perfect stillness

Thus perfect stillness is defined as a return to the natural state

The return to the natural state is called constancy

Understanding constancy is called enlightenment

Not understanding constancy leads to chaos and danger

To understand constancy is to be tolerant

Tolerance leads you to fairness

Fairness leads you to completeness

Completeness leads you to the celestial

The celestial leads you to the Dao

The Dao leads you to the Eternal

And in the Eternal, death holds no fear or danger.

The painting depicts the deities of the Five Planets, which correspond to the five primary elements – wood (Jupiter), fire (Mars), earth (Saturn), metal (Venus) and water (Mercury) – and the 28 constellations of the Chinese zodiac (by Qiu Ying, 16th century).

A painting of Daoist immortal Huang Chuping (by Totoya Hokkei, 1823).

CHAPTER 17

The Natural Order

太上，下知有之；其次，親而譽之；其次，畏之；其次，侮之。信不足焉，有不信焉。悠兮，其貴言。功成事遂，百姓皆謂我自然。

The highest rank of ruler transcends recognition
The next rank is cherished and celebrated
The next is feared
The next is held in contempt:
If the ruler himself has no faith
Then people will have no faith in him
If a ruler is at ease with himself
He chooses his orders carefully
Achievement and success will follow
And the people will accept the natural order.

Scene from a Daoist legend showing keepers of the world and various deities (scroll painting, 17th–18th century).

CHAPTER 18

Neglecting the Dao

大道廢，有仁義；智慧出，有大偽；六親不和，有孝慈；國家昏亂，有忠臣。

If the Dao is neglected
We can turn to Benevolence and Righteousness[7]
If human wit comes to the fore
It brings with it deceit and hypocrisy
If the six relationships fall out of harmony
We can turn to Filial Piety and Charity
If the state falls into disorder
Loyal ministers will come to the fore.

---

[7] Two of the Confucian virtues, along with Filial Piety mentioned further down. Missing is li – Propriety or Observance. In as much as Laozi actually existed, he was contemporary with Confucius, and is mentioned favourably in the latter's writings.

CHAPTER 19

Diminishing the Self

絕聖棄智，民利百倍；絕仁棄義，民復孝慈；絕巧棄利，盜賊無有。此三者以為文不足。故令有所屬：見素抱樸，少私寡欲。

Renounce the sacred wisdom and abandon knowledge
The people will profit a hundredfold
Renounce Benevolence and abandon Righteousness
The people will return to Filial Piety and Charity
Renounce ingenuity and abandon profit
There will be no more robbery and theft
These three propositions are not doctrine enough by themselves
We must also follow these precepts:
Look to the simple and treasure the straightforward
Diminish the self and control desire.

A sumi-e artwork of a beautiful blooming white lotus flower with big leaves and a bud. The white lotus is a symbol of purity.

CHAPTER 20

Different from Others

絕學無憂，唯之與阿，相去幾何？善之與惡，相去若何？人之所畏，不可不畏。荒兮其未央哉！眾人熙熙，如享太牢，如春登臺。我獨怕兮其未兆；如嬰兒之未孩；儽儽兮若無所歸。眾人皆有餘，而我獨若遺。我愚人之心也哉！沌沌兮，俗人昭昭，我獨若昏。俗人察察，我獨悶悶。澹兮其若海，飂兮若無止，眾人皆有以，而我 獨頑似鄙。我獨異於人，而貴食母。

Renouncing learning will bring freedom from worry

What does it matter whether you answer one thing or another

How much difference is there truly between the beautiful and the ugly

The things that people fear should indeed be feared

And how numerous they are!

Other people rejoice and make merry, as though they were enjoying a fine banquet, or admiring the view on a Spring morning

But I remain uncertain and uncommitted, like a baby that has not yet learnt to smile

Exhausted like a traveller with no home to return to

Other people always seem to have more than they need, but I alone never have enough

My thoughts are those of a dullard, other people have clarity

My thoughts are muddy and opaque, whilst other people are keen and open

But I alone am dull and stuffy

I am still as the boundless ocean

Restless as the wind

Other people have a purpose

But I alone am wayward and unformed

I alone am different from others

For I am nurtured by the Dao.

'Spring at the River', a painting by Fan Qui (1646).

'Traveling Amid Streams and Mountains', by Liu Yu (1680).

CHAPTER 21

The Origin of All Things

孔德之容，唯道是從。道之為物，唯恍唯惚。忽兮恍兮，其中有象；恍兮忽兮，其中有物。窈兮冥兮，其中有精；其精甚真，其中有信。自古及今，其名不去，以閱眾甫。吾何以知眾甫之狀哉？以此。

Great Virtue takes its form from the Dao
And the Dao is vague and insubstantial

So vague so insubstantial and yet it has form
So vague so insubstantial and yet it has substance

So deep so dark and yet within is the essence of life
This essence is real and within it is Truth
Throughout time the name of the Dao is constant
And through it I can discern the origin of all things
How can I discern the origin of all things?
From this; from the Dao.

CHAPTER 22

Restraint and Completion

曲則全，枉則直，窪則盈，敝則新，少則得，多則惑。是以聖人抱一為天下式。不自見，故明；不自是，故彰；不自伐，故有功；不自矜，故長。夫唯不爭，故天下莫能與之爭。古之所謂曲則全者，豈虛言哉？誠全而歸之。

The incomplete becomes complete

The crooked becomes straight

The empty is filled

The worn out renewed

Small ambitions are achieved

Great ones are confounded

The enlightened man embraces the Dao and becomes an example for the world

He eschews display and therefore shines

He discards self and so becomes a model

He is self-effacing and therefore achieves recognition

He does not boast and so is celebrated

Because he avoids conflict

No-one under Heaven can find themselves in conflict with him

Who can doubt the truth of the ancient wisdom "The incomplete becomes complete"?

And in completion we return to our true state.

The Legendary Emperor Yao, hanging silk scroll depicting the emperor in a pao, *or robe, by Ma Lin (c. 1194–1264).*

'Snow Landscape', by Hashimoto Gaho (1835-1908).

CHAPTER 23

Trust in the Dao

希言自然，故飄風不終朝，驟雨不終日。孰為此者？天地。天地尚不能久，而況於人乎？故從事於道者，道者，同於道；德者，同於德；失者，同於失。同於道者，道亦樂得之；同於德者，德亦樂得之；同於失者，失亦樂得之。信不足焉，有不信焉。

Nature's way is sparing with words

A whirlwind does not last even a whole morning

Nor a thunderstorm all day

Where do whirlwinds and thunderstorms come from?

They are products of Heaven and Earth

And if these natural phenomena are only short-lived

Why should Man be different?

Thus those who follow the Dao in their actions

Are in accord with the Dao

Those who apply Virtue

Are in accord with Virtue

Those who have lost touch with Virtue and the Dao

Are only in accord with loss.

Those in accord with the Dao
The Dao receives them joyously
Those in accord with Virtue
Virtue receives them joyously
Those in accord with loss
Loss receives them equally joyously
If your trust is not enough
There will be no trust in you.

CHAPTER 24

Left-over Food & Aimless Journeys

企者不立；跨者不行；自見者不明；自是者不彰；自伐者無功；自矜者不長。其在道也，曰：餘食贅行。物或惡之，故有道者不處。

You cannot stand firm on tiptoe
You cannot walk straight with your legs wide apart
A man who prizes display will not shine
A man who exalts himself cannot serve as a model
A man who pushes himself forward will not achieve recognition
A man who boasts will not be celebrated
In terms of the Dao
They are like left-over food and aimless journeys
These actions are odious to the natural order
A true follower of the Dao eschews them.

'Man on a Bridge', 1889. Ren Yi, like his contemporary and friend Xugu (1823–1896), experimented with the realistic rendering of natural scenery instead of producing traditional landscapes composed of conventional compositions and brushstroke formulas. Here, he used irregular patches of wash and hatching to convey the impression of naked branches.

CHAPTER 25

Natural Order

有物混成，先天地生。寂兮寥兮，獨立不改，周行而不殆，可以為天下母。吾不知其名，强字之曰道，强為之名曰大。大曰逝，逝曰遠，遠曰反。故道大，天大，地大，人亦大。域中有四大，而人居其一焉。人法地，地法天，天法道，道法自然。

There is something born of chaos
Created before Heaven and Earth
Voiceless
Formless
It stands alone, unchanging
Ceaselessly circling
The Mother of Creation
I do not know its name
But conscious of my temerity, I call it the Dao
Conscious of my temerity, I call it Great
Calling it Great is also to say it is in motion
Saying it is in motion is to say it travels far
To say it travels far is to say it returns to itself
Thus the Dao is Great
Heaven is Great

Earth is Great

Mankind is Great

Within the Universe there are four Greats

And mankind is one of them

Mankind is governed by Earth

Earth is governed by Heaven

Heaven is governed by the Dao

The Dao is governed by the Natural Order.

CHAPTER 26

Gravity and Temperance

重為輕根，靜為躁君。是以君子終日行不離輜重。雖有榮觀，燕處超然。奈何萬乘之主，而以身輕天下？輕則失本，躁則失君。

Heaviness is the foundation of lightness

Quiescence is the master of activity

So when a nobleman is on his travels

Not for one moment during the day does he let his baggage train out of his sight

Even in the most beautiful scenery

He remains calm and dispassionate

How much the less then may a lord of 10,000 chariots

Treat his subjects lightly

Through lightness he loses his foundation

Through intemperance he loses his throne.

CHAPTER 27

Deftness and Enlightenment

善行無轍跡，善言無瑕讁；善數不用籌策；善閉無關楗而不可開，善結無繩約而不可解。是以聖人常善救人，故無棄人；常善救物，故無棄物。是謂襲明。故善人者，不善人之師；不善人者，善人之資。不貴其師，不愛其資，雖智大迷，是謂要妙。

Skilled carriage-driving leaves no wheel-tracks
Skilled oratory leaves no opening for opponents
Skilled reckoning does not need tallies
A skilfully made door needs no bolts to stop it swinging open
Skilled binding needs no knots but cannot be loosened
Thus the Wise Man excels in the care of his people
And no-one is ever lost to him
He excels in the care of his possessions
And nothing is ever lost to him
In this we may call him enlightened
So the Wise Man is tutor to lesser men
And lesser men are his pupils
For the pupil not to respect his master
And the master not to cherish his pupils
Overrides intelligence and leads only to confusion
This is an essential Mystery of the Dao.

Guan Yu (died AD 219), a warrior of the late Han dynasty (206 BC–AD 220) renowned for his valour and faithfulness, was later venerated as a saint in the Daoist pantheon.

'Mountain Stream on a Summer Day', by Nakabayashi Chikutō.

CHAPTER 28

A River Valley to the World

知其雄，守其雌，為天下谿。為天下谿，常德不離，復歸於嬰兒。知其白，守其黑，為天下式。為天下式，常德不忒，復歸於無極。知其榮，守其辱，為天下谷。為天下谷，常德乃足，復歸於樸。樸散則為器，聖人用之，則為官長，故大制不割。

The man who understands his masculine nature

But also cherishes the feminine

Is like a mountain stream for the world

Like a mountain stream for the world, constant in virtue

He is like a new-born child

If he understands the light

But also cherishes the dark

He serves as a model for the world

As a model for the world, unwavering in virtue

He returns to the Infinite

If he understands renown

But also cherishes abasement

He is like a river valley to the world

As a river valley to the world, complete in virtue

He returns to the unformed state

From the unformed state are formed tools and instruments

The Wise Man uses these to lead his government

So we may see that effective rule requires simple measures.

CHAPTER 29

Avoiding Extremes

將欲取天下而為之，吾見其不得已。天下神器，不可為也，不可執也為者敗之，執者失之。是以聖人無為故無敗無執故無失夫物或行或隨；或歔或吹；或強或羸；或挫或隳。是以聖人去甚，去奢，去泰。

For someone who desires to control the world
I see no chance of success
The world is an instrument of the Spirit
It cannot be controlled
It cannot be grasped
Those who try to control it are defeated
Those who try to grasp it, lose it
So the Wise man seeks not to control
And so is not defeated
Seeks not to grasp
And so cannot lose it
The things in Creation may lead or follow,
Draw in or expel
Grow strong or weaken
Succeed or fail
Thus the Wise Man avoids the extreme
Shuns extravagance
And renounces the arrogant.

A gilt brass sculpture showing the Daoist immortal Laozi, by Chen Yanqing (1438).

Yuding Zhenren was one of the Twelve Golden Xian, 12 of Yuanshi Tianzun's greatest students. He was a devoted follower of Branch Chan of Daoism, fighting against Branch Jie.

CHAPTER 30

Accordance with the Dao

以道佐人主者，不以兵強天下。其事好還。師之所處，荊棘生焉。大軍之後，必有凶年。善有果而已，不敢以取強。果而勿矜，果而勿伐，果而勿驕。果而不得已，果而勿強。物壯則老，是謂不道，不道早已。

Followers of the Dao who wish to help their ruler
Do not do so by force of arms
For such affairs rebound on their authors
Brambles grow where an army has camped
And famine follows a great campaign
Assuring a proper outcome is all that matters
Never force the issue
Once it is achieved, avoid complacency
Once it is achieved, do not be self-satisfied
Once it is achieved, do not show arrogance
What is achieved is dictated only by necessity
And should not be forced beyond what is necessary
Such things take shape and then wither
This not in accordance with the Dao
And what is not in accordance with the Dao, is transient.

CHAPTER 31

The Sorrow of War

夫兵者，不祥之器，物或惡之，故有道者不處。君子居則貴左，用兵則貴右。兵者不祥之器，非君子之器，不得已而用之，恬淡為上。勝而不美。而美之者，是樂 殺人。夫樂殺人者，則不可以得志於天下矣。吉事尚左，凶事尚右。偏將軍居左，上將軍居右，言以喪禮處之。殺人之眾，以哀悲泣之，戰勝以喪禮處之。

Now as to weapons, these are inauspicious tools

Abhorrent to all things

A follower of the Dao has no place for them

In his palace in peacetime, the ruler accords honour and respect to the left-hand side

But in war, it is the right

Weapons are inauspicious tools

They are not the tools of a ruler

And he only turns to them as a last resort

Above all he prizes the quiet and unremarkable

Victory is not something he covets

Since a man who covets victory perforce delights in slaughter

And a man who delights in slaughter will never truly impose his will on the world

In celebration the left is the place of honour
In mourning it is the right
The second-in-command takes his place on the left
The commander on the right
For this is in accordance with the funeral rites
Anyone who has slaughtered a multitude in battle
Should weep for them in bitter mourning
And victory should be marked in accordance with the funeral rites.

This 18th century painting depicts the eminent monk Cheongheodang Hyujeong (1520–1604), better known by his posthumous title Great Master Seosan.

'The Daoist Immortal Liezi' (1606). These panels depict Daoist immortal Liezi, who flies away on a cloud, while awestruck figures discuss his mysterious disappearance. These door panels, or fusuma, originally decorated the west wall in the central room of the abbot's quarters (hōjō) at Ryōanji, a Zen temple in Kyoto. They are part of a set of 40 panels depicting assorted Confucian and Daoist figures that were installed in the three rooms.

CHAPTER 32

The Harmonious Dao

道常，無名，樸。雖小，天下莫能臣。侯王若能守之，萬物將自賓。天地相合，以降甘露，民莫之令而自均。始制有名，名亦既有，夫亦將知止，知止所以不殆。譬道之在天下，猶川谷之與江海。

The Dao is infinite, nameless and unformed
Small it may be, but no-one may master it
Lords and rulers who cherish it
Will bring everything naturally under their dominion
Under its influence Heaven and Earth are in harmony
Sending down a sweet essence
Which spreads evenly beyond man's control.
When control and regulation are initiated we give things names
But in giving names we must know when to stop
For knowing when to stop is our safeguard
We may say that the Dao's relationship to the world is like that of valleys to rivers and rivers to the oceans.

CHAPTER 33

Longevity

知人者智，自知者明。勝人者有力，自勝者強。知足者富。強行者有志。不失其所者久。死而不亡者壽。

Someone who knows men has only knowledge
But to know yourself is perception
Someone who conquers men has only force
But to conquer yourself is true strength
To recognize sufficiency is to be rich
To hold a steadfast course is to have will
Someone who does not lose his place in the world will live long
But one who dies and whose presence remains achieves true longevity.

'Lao Tzu', 1922.

Marshal Wang, one of the guardian deities of Daoism, is charged with protecting Daoist temples. Like many popular Daoist deities, Wang was originally a human who was posthumously revered as a god. Here, he rides a flaming wheel, vanquishing the evil serpent spirits in the river below.

CHAPTER 34

The Pervasive Dao

大道汜兮，其可左右。萬物恃之而生而不辭，功成而不有。衣養萬物而不為主，常無欲，可名於小；萬物歸焉，而不為主，可名為大。以其終不自為大，故能成其大。

How pervasive is the Dao!

Left and right are the same to it

The whole of Creation relies on it to grow and it never refuses

It claims no credit for what it accomplishes

It clothes and feeds but exerts no control

Eternally without desire, in this respect it may be called small

All things return to it but it exerts no control

In this respect it may be called great

Because it places no insistence on its greatness

Greatness is truly what it achieves.

Detail of 'Daoist Deities Visit the Celestial Worthy of the Original Beginning'. Mural from Pure Trinity Hall, Yongle Palace, Shanxi (Yuan Dynasty).

CHAPTER 35

The Inexhaustible Dao

執大象，天下往。往而不害，安平大。樂與餌，過客止。道之出口，淡乎其無味，視之不足見，聽之不足聞，用之不足既。

If you have firm hold of the Dao, all under heaven beat a path to your door
Where they find no harm, only peace and tranquillity
Music and fine food attract the passing guest
However when we speak of the Dao it seems bland and without savour
And yet to look at, to listen to, to use, it is inexhaustible.

CHAPTER 36

Maintaining the Mystery of the Dao

將欲歙之，必固張之；將欲弱之，必固強之；將欲廢之，必固興之；將欲奪之，必固與之。是謂微明。柔弱勝剛強。魚不可脫於淵，國之利器不可以示人。

That which is to be shrunk must first be stretched
That which is to be weakened must first be made strong
That which is to be overthrown must first be established
That which is to be taken away must first be given
This is an essential Mystery of the Dao
Soft and supple overcome strong and firm
A fish cannot leave the water
The State's most effective tool should not be revealed to its people.

'The Pleasures of Fishes', by Zhou Dongqing (late 13th century), Yuan Dynasty.

'Guanyin as Guide of Souls', Tang Dynasty silk banner from the Mogao Caves, Dunhuang, Gansu Province, 10th century.

CHAPTER 37

Tranquillity

道常無為而無不為。侯王若能守之，萬物將自化。化而欲作，吾將鎮之以無名之樸。夫亦將無欲。不欲以靜，天下將自定。

The Dao is eternally without action yet there is nothing it does not achieve
If rulers embrace it, all things will transform of their own accord
Should this transformation give rise to desire
It will be quelled by the nameless and unformed Dao
And there will be no desire
In the absence of desire there will be tranquillity
And the world will settle into its proper form.

CHAPTER 38

Avoidance of Chaos

上德不德，是以有德；下德不失德，是以無德。上德無為而無以為；下德為之而有以為。上仁為之而無以為；上義為之而有以為。上禮為之而莫之應，則攘臂而扔之。故失道而後德，失德而後仁，失仁而後義，失義而後禮。夫禮者，忠信之薄，而亂之首。前識者，道之華，而愚之始。是以大丈夫處其厚，不居其薄；處其實，不居其華。故去彼取此。

The highest Virtue does not flaunt itself, and thus is retained
The lowest Virtue seeks to preserve itself, and thus is lost
The highest Virtue is naturally without action and thus needs no action
The lowest Virtue acts and thus needs to act
The highest Benevolence is naturally so, and has no need to practice benevolence
The highest Righteousness is naturally so, and must act upon itself
The highest Propriety is naturally so
And if it is not reciprocated, it will enforce itself
When the Dao is lost it is replaced by Virtue
When Virtue is lost it is replaced by Benevolence.
When Benevolence is lost it is replaced by Righteousness

When Righteousness is lost it is replaced by Propriety
When Propriety is lost through lack of loyalty and good faith
It is the beginning of chaos
Prescience is a mere embellishment of the Dao
And leads to stupidity
Thus a worthy man relies on his strengths
And avoids his weaknesses
He embraces the former and discards the latter.

Frieze showing Dao deities and figures at Ming Sheng Gung Tao temple in Xian, China.

'The Jade Purity', first of the Three Pure Ones (Sanqing) in Daoism. Hanging scroll painting, 19th century.

CHAPTER 39

Wisdom of the Ancients

昔之得一者：天得一以清；地得一以寧；神得一以靈；谷得一以盈；萬物得一以生；侯王得一以為天下貞。其致之也謂：天無以清，將恐裂；地無以寧，將恐發；神無以靈，將恐歇；谷無以盈，將恐竭；萬物無以生，將恐滅；侯王無以貴高將恐蹶。故貴以賤為本，高以下為基。是以侯王自稱孤、寡、不穀。此非以賤為本耶？非乎？故致數譽無譽。不欲琭琭如玉，珞珞如石。

In ancient times, understanding of the Dao progressed thus:
It brought clarity to Heaven
It brought stability to Earth
It breathed soul into the spirits
Brought fertility to the valleys
Gave life to all Creation
And made rulers models for the world
From this we can go on to say:
Without clarity Heaven would collapse
Without stability Earth would crumble.
Without soul the spirits would disappear

Without fertility the valleys would shrivel
Without life Creation would be extinguished
And unless they are exalted, rulers would fall
Thus the exalted takes humility as its foundation
The lofty takes the lowly as its base
For this reason, rulers call themselves lowly, humble and without ambition
For is this not indeed taking humility as their foundation?
Thus they know that a multitude of honours do not themselves bring honour
They do not aspire to the elegance of fine jade
But to the ordinariness of stone.

CHAPTER 40

Non-being

反者道之動；弱者道之用。天下萬物生於有，有生於無。

The Dao moves in an endless cycle
It is yielding in its method
All things come from being
And being comes from non-being.

An 18th century scroll painting showing the Daoist pantheon.

CHAPTER 41

The Paradox of the Dao

上士聞道，勤而行之；中士聞道，若存若亡；下士聞道，大笑之。不笑不足以為道。故建言有之：明道若昧；進道若退；夷道若纇；上德若谷；大白若辱；廣德若不足；建德若偷；質真若渝；大方無隅；大器晚成；大音希聲；大象無形；道隱無名。夫唯道，善貸且成。

The superior scholar listens to the Dao and puts it into practice

The middling scholar listens to the Dao and sometimes practices it and sometimes forgets it

The inferior scholar listens to the Dao and laughs at it –

Without their laughter it could not be the Dao

As the ancient wisdom says:

In its brightness the Dao seems dull

In advancing it seems to retreat

In its openness it appears complicated

Its greatest virtue is like an empty valley

Its purity seems blemished

The expanse of its virtue seems inadequate

Its probity seems dishonest.

Its solid truth seems elusive
Like a square without corners
A tool that arrives too late
A great sound with little noise
A great image without form
The Dao is hidden and without a name
Yet it is the Dao that can bring fulfilment to all things.

Chinese Emperor Fu Hsi, wearing traditional costume, holding the 'Yin-yang' symbol.

CHAPTER 42

The Basis of My Teaching

道生一，一生二，二生三，三生萬物。萬物負陰而抱陽，沖氣以為和。人之所惡，唯孤、寡、不穀，而王公以為稱。故物或損之而益，或益之而損。人之所教，我亦教之。強梁者不得其死，吾將以為教父。

The Basis of My Teaching
The Dao begets unity
Unity begets duality
Duality begets trinity
Trinity begets Creation
Creation is bound up in Yin and Yang
Whose swirling energies combine
Words that ordinary people disdain:
Lowly, humble, without ambition
Are those that rulers use to describe themselves
Thus one may benefit from another's loss
Or lose to another's benefit
What others teach, I also teach
Tyrants do not die a natural death
This is the basis of my teaching.

CHAPTER 43

Achieved by Very Few

天下之至柔，馳騁天下之至堅。無有入無間，吾是以知無為之有益。不言之教，無為之益，天下希及之。

The softest things on Earth
Overcome the hardest
The insubstantial can penetrate even where there are no openings
This is how I understand the benefits of Not-Doing
Teaching without words
And the benefits of Not-Doing
Are things achieved by very few.

'Spring Dawn Over the Elixir Terrace', by Lu Guang (1369).

'Great Emperor of Longevity of the South Pole'. Third of the Four Heavenly Ministers of Daoism.

CHAPTER 44

Ensuring Longevity

名與身孰親？身與貨孰多？得與亡孰病？是故甚愛必大費；多藏必厚亡。知足不辱，知止不殆，可以長久。

Fame or health, which is more dear?
Health or wealth, which is worth more?
Gain or loss, which is more harmful?
Excessive love carries a heavy price
Covetousness brings ruin
Recognizing sufficiency and knowing when to stop
Avoids these consequences
And ensures longevity.

The Three Pure Ones, the highest gods in the Daoist pantheon. Site of Baodingshan (1179–1249).

CHAPTER 45

Order Under Heaven

大成若缺，其用不弊。大盈若沖，其用不窮。大直若屈，大巧若拙，大辯若訥。躁勝寒靜勝熱。清靜為天下正。

The greatest achievement may seem unfinished
But its application is endless
Total fullness may seem empty
But its application is endless
Total rectitude may seem crooked
The greatest skill may seem clumsy
The highest eloquence may seem tongue-tied
Activity overcomes cold
Stillness overcomes heat
Tranquillity brings order under Heaven.

CHAPTER 46

At One With the Dao

天下有道，卻走馬以糞。天下無道，戎馬生於郊。禍莫大於不知足；咎莫大於欲得。故知足之足，常足矣。

In a world at one with the Dao
Carriage horses fertilize the fields
In a world without the Dao
War-horses are bred at the frontier
No disaster is worse than not recognizing sufficiency
No crime is greater than acquisitiveness
Thus recognizing the sufficiency of sufficiency
Is eternally sufficient.

A leading horse painter of the Tang dynasty, Han Gan was known for capturing not only the likeness of a horse but also its spirit. This painting, the most famous work attributed to the artist, is a portrait of a charger of Emperor Xuanzong (r. 712–56). With its burning eye, flaring nostrils and dancing hoofs, the fiery-tempered horse epitomizes Chinese myths about Central Asian 'celestial steeds' that 'sweated blood' and were actually dragons in disguise.

CHAPTER 47

Knowing Without Moving

不出戶知天下；不闚牖見天道。其出彌遠，其知彌少。是以聖人不行而知，不見而名，不為而成。

Without leaving one's door one can know the world
Without looking out of the window one can understand the Dao of Heaven
The further one travels the less one knows
Thus the enlightened man can know without moving
Name without seeing
Accomplish without doing.

CHAPTER 48

Loss Upon Loss

為學日益，為道日損。損之又損，以至於無為。無為而無不為。取天下常以無事，及其有事，不足以取天下。

Through study one adds knowledge daily
In practising the Dao one subtracts daily
Loss upon loss until one reaches a state of Not-Doing
Through Not-Doing everything may be done
The empire is won by not interfering
Interfere and the empire will never be won.

Wenchang Wang is the Daoist deity of culture and literature.

CHAPTER 49

The Enlightened Man

聖人無常心，以百姓心為心。善者，吾善之；不善者，吾亦善之；德善。信者，吾信之；不信者，吾亦信之；德信。聖人在天下，歙歙為天下渾其心，百姓皆注其耳目，聖人皆孩之。

The enlightened man has no will of his own
He follows the will of the people
I am kind to those who are kind themselves
I am also kind to the unkind
The Virtue of kindness
I trust those who themselves trust
I also trust those who have no trust
The Virtue of trust
The enlightened man goes gently in the world
Tempering his mind to it
The people all look to his deeds and listen to his words
And he treats them all as his children.

CHAPTER 50

Life and Death

出生入死。生之徒，十有三；死之徒，十有三；人之生，動之死地，十有三。夫何故？以其生，生之厚。蓋聞善攝生者，陸行不遇兕虎，入軍不被甲兵；兕無所投其角，虎無所措其爪，兵無所容其刃。夫何故？以其無死地。

We may expect three in ten to live out their natural life

Three in ten to die an untimely death

And three in ten will live precariously at risk of death

Why is this? Because they value their life too highly

I have heard it said that those who manage the life they are given well

Can travel without threat from rhinoceros or tiger[8]

And can fight in an army without armour or weapon

The rhinoceros finds no place to thrust its horn

The tiger finds no place to gouge its claws

The weapon no place for its point to pierce

Why is this? Because death has no place in them.

---

[8] Both rhino and tiger were native to ancient China. Rhino hunts are described in the earliest form of Chinese writing on oracle bones dating from the Shang Dynasty (16th–11th c BCE), and the beasts themselves are depicted in bronze from that period on. They are now extinct. The South China Tiger is also probably extinct in the wild now, but survives in captivity. Its range used to be from the Yellow River valley to the South China Sea, and its symbolism to the Chinese is almost as powerful as the dragon's.

Huang Chuping was the human form of the Daoist deity Huang Daxian, which translates as 'Great Immortal Huang'. Huang Chuping was a Daoist hermit from Zheijang, born in AD 238. Huang Chuping was said to have experienced great hunger and poverty in his youth, becoming a shepherd by his eighth birthday. One day, when he was 15 years old, he met an immortal on Red Pine Mountain, and began practising Daoism as a result.

'Hotei Crossing a Stream' (by Fūgai Ekun, 1650).

CHAPTER 51

The Mysterious Process

道生之，德畜之，物形之，勢成之。是以萬物莫不尊道而貴德。道之尊，德之貴，夫莫之命而常自然。故道生之，德畜之；長之育之；亭之毒之；養之覆之。生而不有，為而不恃，長而不宰，是謂玄德。

The Dao produces
Virtue nurtures
Substance gives form
Circumstance complete
Thus everything in Creation reveres the Dao and honours Virtue
Reverence for the Dao and honour for Virtue
Are not observed by command, it is the eternal natural way
The Dao produces
And Virtue nurtures, raises, educates, shelters, heals, feeds and protects
Producing without owning
Doing without claiming credit
Rearing but not slaughtering
This is the mystery of Virtue.

CHAPTER 52

Understanding the Infinite

天下有始，以為天下母。既得其母，以知其子，既知其子，復守其母，沒身不殆。塞其兌，閉其門，終身不勤。開其兌，濟其事，終身不救。見小曰明，守柔曰強。用其光，復歸其明，無遺身殃；是為習常。

The world had its origin in the Dao
Which may be considered as its mother
By knowing the mother you can know the child
By knowing the child, you cherish the mother the more
And even death holds no fear
Close your eyes and ears to the sights and sounds of the world
And your life will be easy
Open your mouth
And meddle with affairs
And life will be a perpetual struggle
To recognize the importance of the small is called clarity
To nurture the weak is called strength
Use the illumination of the Dao to find clarity
And avoid harm
This is to understand the Infinite.

A mother holds her child (17th century Japanese scroll).

'Drunk in Autumn Woods', by Zhu Ruoji (1702).

CHAPTER 53

The Winding By-ways

使我介然有知，行於大道，唯施是畏。
大道甚夷，而民好徑。朝甚除，田甚
蕪，倉甚虛；服文綵，帶利劍，厭飲
食，財貨有餘；是謂盜夸。非道也哉！

Should I suddenly find myself in a position
To govern according to the Dao
I would only have one cause for concern
The Dao, is straight and easy
But people prefer the winding by-ways
The courtyards of their mansions may be fine and well-kept
But the fields are untilled
And the granaries empty
They wear fine clothes
Carry sharp swords
Gorge themselves on food and drink
Hoard their extravagant possessions
But this just makes them thieves and plunderers
This is most assuredly not in accord with the Dao!

CHAPTER 54

Cultivating Virtue

善建不拔，善抱者不脫，子孫以祭祀不輟。修之於身，其德乃真；修之於家，其德乃餘；修之於鄉，其德乃長；修之於國，其德乃豐；修之於天下，其德乃普。故以身觀身，以家觀家，以鄉觀鄉，以國觀國，以天下觀天下。吾何以知天下然哉？以此。

What is well founded cannot be uprooted
What is well protected cannot be torn away
Sons and grandsons maintain the ancestral rites
If the Dao is cultivated by an individual
His Virtue is constant
If it is cultivated in a household
Its Virtue overflows
If it is cultivated in a village
Its Virtue is long long-lasting
If it is cultivated in a state
Its Virtue will flourish
If it is cultivated in the world
Its virtue is universal
Thus an individual should be judged as an individual
A household as a household
A village as a village
A state as a state
And the world as the world
How can I know this about the world?
From the process I have just described!

'Landscapes of the Four Seasons', by Zhu Ruoji.

'Palace Ladies Bathing Children', 11th century, Song dynasty (960-1279).

CHAPTER 55

Purity of the New-Born

含德之厚，比於赤子。蜂蠆虺蛇不螫，猛獸不據，攫鳥不搏。骨弱筋柔而握固。未知牝牡之合而全作，精之至也。終日號而不嗄，和之至也。知和曰常，知常曰明，益生曰祥。心使氣曰強。物壯則老，謂之不道，不道早已。

We should measure our virtue against that of a new-born child
Neither hornets nor scorpions nor snakes will sting an infant
Savage beasts will not attack it
Birds of prey will not swoop on it
Its bones and sinews are soft, but its grip is strong
It has no knowledge of sexual union
But its penis is already primed
Because of the purity of its physical essence
It can cry all day but not go hoarse
Because of its physical harmony
To know harmony is called constancy
To know constancy is called clarity
But self-indulgence may be called ill-omened
And wilfulness may be called over-bearing
For things taken to the extreme will then decline
And this is not in accord with the Dao
What is not in accord with the Dao soon withers and dies.

CHAPTER 56

Honouring the Dao

知者不言，言者不知。塞其兑，閉其門，挫其銳，解其分，和其光，同其塵，是謂玄同。故不可得而親，不可得而疏；不可得而利，不可得而害；不可得而貴，不可得而賤。故為天下貴。

A wise man speaks little
A garrulous man is not wise
Block the openings
Shut the doors
Blunt the edges
Loosen the knots
Soften the glare
Settle the dust
This is the Mysterious Unity
The Dao brings neither closeness nor separation
Neither profit nor harm
Neither honour nor disgrace
For this reason it is honoured above all other things.

Detail showing Northern Qi scholars collating the classic texts, traditionally attributed to Yen Li-pen.

CHAPTER 57

Benefits of Simplicity

以正治國，以奇用兵，以無事取天下。吾何以知其然哉？以此：天下多忌諱，而民彌貧；人多利器，國家滋昏；人多伎巧，奇物滋起；法令滋彰，盜賊多有。故聖人云：我無為，而民自化；我好靜，而民自正；我無事，而民自富；我無欲，而民自樸。

Be orthodox in governing the state
But unorthodox in war
Win the world by being uninvolved
How do I know this?
By this:
The more restrictions that are placed on the empire
The poorer the people become
The better the weapons the people carry
The more disordered the state
The more skilful the craftsmen
The more devious and pernicious their products
The more intrusive the legal system
The more thieves and robbers you'll find
Thus the enlightened man says:
I practice non-action

And the people will transform themselves

I embrace tranquillity

And the people will order themselves

I remain uninvolved

And the people will prosper

I keep myself free from desire

And the people will find simplicity.

'The Simple Retreat', by Wang Meng (1370).

CHAPTER 58

Sharp but Not Dangerous

其政悶悶，其民淳淳；其政察察，其民缺缺。禍兮福之所倚，福兮禍之所伏。孰知其極？其無正。正復為奇，善復為妖。人之迷，其日固久。是以聖人方而不割，廉而不劌，直而不肆，光而不燿。

If government is subdued
The people will be honest
If government is obtrusive
The people will be discontent
Misery and happiness are inter-dependent
And one hides behind the other
Who knows their limits?
Without the orthodox
The unorthodox takes over
And good turns to bad
This befuddles the people
With enduring confusion
So the enlightened man stands four-square without causing harm
Is sharp but not dangerous
Is straight but does not over-extend
Shines but does not dazzle.

A scene from 'The Sixteen Luohans', by Chen Xian. Chen Xian was a Buddhist monk who painted mostly religious figures. In the chaos that accompanied the fall of the Ming dynasty in 1644, many Buddhist monks left China for Japan, and some brought paintings by Chen, which found favour. For this reason, he is better known in Japan than in his native country.

Han Xiangzi is a Chinese mythological character and one of the Eight Immortals. Han Xiangzi is believed to have been known as Han Xiang before his immortality, and was born in the Tang Dynasty, the grandnephew of promiment poet and scholar Han Yu. Han Xiangzi became an immortal under the tutelage of Lu Dongbin, another of the Eight Immortals, who taught him the Daoist magical arts that would eventually lead to his apotheosis and immortality.

CHAPTER 59

Thrift

治人事天莫若嗇。夫唯嗇，是謂早服；早服謂之重積德；重積德則無不克；無不克則莫知其極；莫知其極，可以有國；有國之母，可以長久；是謂深根固柢，長生久視之道。

In governing the people and serving heaven
Nothing compares to thrift
It is only by thrift that one can be prepared
In being prepared one accumulates virtue
By accumulating virtue every obstacle is overcome
In overcoming every obstacle all limits are removed
Knowing no limits, one may attain the empire
In being the foundation of the empire, one may endure
This is known as having deep roots and a sturdy trunk
It is the enduring and visionary Dao.

A stone engraving of the Five Sacred Mountains, Song dynasty (960–1279).

CHAPTER 60

Doing No Harm

治大國若烹小鮮。以道蒞天下，其鬼不神；非其鬼不神，其神不傷人；非其神不傷人，聖人亦不傷人。夫兩不相傷，故德交歸焉。

Governing the state is like cooking a small fish[9]
When the Dao orders the world
The spirits do not manifest themselves
It is not just that they do not manifest themselves
But that they will do no harm
It is not just that the spirits will do no harm
The enlightened man will also do no harm
When neither does harm
Virtue is able to expand.

[9] If you keep messing with it, it will disintegrate.

'Sun and Moon over Land and Sea' (Ming dynasty, 1368–1644).

CHAPTER 61

The Power of Receptiveness

大國者下流，天下之交，天下之牝。牝常以靜勝牡，以靜為下。故大國以下小國，則取小國；小國以下大國，則取大國。故或下以取，或下而取。大國不過欲兼畜人，小國不過欲入事人。夫兩者各得其所欲，大者宜為下。

A great state is like the ocean receiving the rivers
In the intercourse of the world, it takes the female part
The female eternally subdues the male through passivity
In passivity it is receptive
Thus a great state wins over smaller states by making itself receptive to them
And a small state may win over a great state by its receptive nature
In the one case receptiveness is the tool
In the other it is the reason
A great state desires to unite and satisfy its people
A small state desires only to be received and enter into service
Thus each gets what it desires
And it behoves a great state to be receptive.

CHAPTER 62

Honouring the Dao

道者萬物之奧。善人之寶，不善人之所保。美言可以市，尊行可以加人。人之不善，何棄之有？故立天子，置三公，雖有拱璧以先駟馬，不如坐進此道。古之所以貴此道者何？不曰：以求得，有罪以免耶？故為天下貴。

The Dao is the great mystery of Creation
It is a treasure to the good
And a refuge to the bad
Noble words can bring respect
Noble deeds can bring advancement
But what of the bad man?
How could it be that the Dao is denied to him!
Thus when the Son of Heaven is enthroned
And the three Dukes enfeoffed
Even the ordained offerings of jade discs and 4-horse chariots
Are as nothing compared to sitting before them and expounding the Dao
What of those ancients who thus honoured the Dao?
Did they not say that those who sought it would attain it?
And those who transgressed would be pardoned?
For this reason it is honoured above all other things.

This depiction of Daoist deities from 1454 was once part of a set of paintings used in the Buddhist water-and-land ritual. The identity of the deities is given in an inscription: "Portrait of the Northern Dipper, Central Dipper, and Root Destiny Star Lords."

CHAPTER 63

By Means of the Dao

為無為，事無事，味無味。大小多少，報怨以德。圖難於其易，為大於其細；天下難事，必作於易，天下大事，必作於細。是以聖人終不為大，故能成其大。夫輕諾必寡信，多易必多難。是以聖人猶難之，故終無難矣。

Through the Dao: one does through Not-doing

Manages by not intervening

Tastes by not tasting

Big, small, many, few make no difference

Enmity is met with Virtue

Plan for the difficult while it is still easy

Act on a grand scale while it is still small

The most difficult tasks in the world

Must be started when they are easy

The biggest tasks in the world

Must be started when they are small

This is how the enlightened man need never act on a grand scale

But is able to achieve great things

One who makes promises easily is unlikely to keep them

And one who treats matters lightly is bound to find them difficult

This is why the enlightened man treats everything as difficult

And in the end faces no difficulty at all.

CHAPTER 64

Being Cautious

其安易持，其未兆易謀。其脆易泮，其微易散。為之於未有，治之於未亂。合抱之木，生於毫末；九層之臺，起於累土；千里之行，始於足下。為者敗之，執者失之。是以聖人無為故無敗；無執故無失。民之從事，常於幾成而敗之。慎終如始，則無敗事，是以聖人欲不欲，不貴難得之貨；學不學，復眾人之所過，以輔萬物之自然，而不敢為。

Things are easy to handle in times of peace
And easy to plan against if there are no bad omens
The fragile is easily broken
The small is easily dispersed
Act before it becomes established
Govern before confusion sets in
A tree whose trunk your arms can only just encircle
Starts out as a sapling
A nine-storey platform[10]
Starts out as a mound of earth
A journey of a thousand *li*
Starts where you stand

---

[10] It was customary for rulers to conduct important ceremonies on raised stages in their palace courtyards. Nine is the number of the highest earthly, as opposed to heavenly, authority.

Lao Tzu riding a water buffalo, from a 19th century engraving.

By acting you fail

In grasping you lose

Thus the enlightened man acts through Not-doing

And so cannot fail

Does not grasp and so does not lose

The affairs of the people are often lost just at the point of success

But if you are as cautious throughout as you are at the outset

Affairs will not be lost

Thus the enlightened man desires the absence of desire

And sets no store by the rare and precious

He learns through not studying

Pays attention to what the common people ignore

And thereby helps things find their true nature

Whilst not himself daring to act.

The Jade Emperor is one of the most important deities in Daoism. He is considered the ruler of heaven and a manifestation of the first god.

The Great Congruence of the Dao

古之善為道者，非以明民，將以愚之。民之難治，以其智多。故以智治國，國之賊；不以智治國，國之福。知此兩者亦稽式。常知稽式，是謂玄德。玄德深矣，遠矣，與物反矣，然後乃至大順。

In ancient times, those adepts of the Dao
Did not seek to enlighten the people
But sought to dull their understanding
A knowledgeable population is hard to govern
Thus a ruler who disseminates knowledge to rule
Brings disaster to his country
A ruler who keeps his people uninformed
Brings prosperity
Someone who understands these two principles will take them as his guide
To be constant in this model is what is called the deep Virtue of the Dao
This Virtue is profound and far-reaching
It leads things to return to their original state
Until eventually they reach the Great Congruence of the Dao.

CHAPTER 66

Taking the Lower Position

江海所以能為百谷王者，以其善下之，故能為百谷王。是以聖人欲上民，必以言下之；欲先民，必以身後之。是以聖人處上而民不重，處前而民不害。是以天下樂推而不厭。以其不爭，故天下莫能與之爭。

The reason why the rivers and oceans are lords of the valleys and streams
Is because they occupy the lower position
This is why they can rule over them
For the same reason, an enlightened man who wishes to rule over the people
Must, in his speech, take the humbler position
If he wishes to lead them, he takes his place behind them
In this way, although he is above them, he does not oppress them
And although he leads them, he does not lead them into harm
Thus the world delights in his rule and does not tire of it
Because he is in conflict with no-one
No-one can be in conflict with him.

'River Landscape with Fireflies', 1874.

Lan Caihe is a Chinese mythological character and one of the Eight Immortals.

CHAPTER 67

Three Treasures

天下皆謂我道大，似不肖。夫唯大，故似不肖。若肖久矣。其細也夫！我有三寶，持而保之。一曰慈，二曰儉，三曰不敢為天下先。慈故能勇；儉故能廣；不敢為天下先，故能成器長。今舍慈且勇；舍儉且廣；舍後且先；死矣！夫慈以戰則勝，以守則固。天將救之，以慈衛之。

All the world calls my Dao great, and unlike anything else

It is indeed because of its greatness that it resembles no other teaching

If it did resemble any other

It would have diminished

I have three treasures that I cleave to and cherish

The first is gentleness

The second is frugality

And the third is that I do not place myself ahead of the world

Because I am gentle I can be bold

Because I am frugal I can be liberal

And because I do not place myself first

My usefulness is abiding

Nowadays, people put boldness before gentleness

Liberality before frugality

And put themselves first rather than last

This is fatal!

For gentleness will surely prevail in the battle

And steadfastly hold its ground

Heaven will protect the gentle

By means of their own gentleness.

CHAPTER 68

Following the Ancient Wisdom

善為士者，不武；善戰者，不怒；善勝敵者，不與；善用人者，為之下。是謂不爭之德，是謂用人之力，是謂配天古之極。

A good officer is not aggressive
A good warrior does not lose his temper
Those skilled in victory do not actually engage the enemy
A good employer adopts a humble posture
This is called the virtue of non-contention
It is also known as the potential of employment
And may be called following the ancient wisdom.

An immortal of the Daoist religion (ink on paper, Yuan dynasty).

'Chinese Sage Evoking a Dragon', c. 1825.

CHAPTER 69

Regretting Aggression

用兵有言：吾不敢為主，而為客；不敢進寸，而退尺。是謂行無行；攘無臂；扔無敵；執無兵。禍莫大於輕敵，輕敵幾喪吾寶。故抗兵相加，哀者勝矣。

There is an axiom of military strategy:
I prefer to be the guest rather than the host
I prefer to retreat a foot than advance an inch
This is acting without moving
Fighting without baring one's arms
Advancing where there is no enemy
Grasping no weapon
There is no calamity worse than thoughtlessly going to war
For in doing so I lose that which is most precious to me
Thus when two sides do actually engage
The one that does so with regret will be the victor.

CHAPTER 70

A Precious Jade

吾言甚易知，甚易行。天下莫能知，莫能行。言有宗，事有君。夫唯無知，是以不我知。知我者希，則我者貴。是以聖人被褐懷玉。

My words are easy to understand
And easy to put into practice
Yet no-one in the world understands them
And no-one puts them into practice
My words have their principles and my actions their governance
If people do not understand this, they cannot understand me
The fewer people who understand me, the more worthy I am of honour
Thus the enlightened man may wear clothes of coarse weave, but he has a precious jade at his breast.

Daoist Immortal with Dragon (19th century).

'Descending Geese', by Japanese artist Unkoku Togan (1547–1618).

CHAPTER 71

Recognizing One's Faults

知不知上；不知知病。夫唯病病，是以不病。聖人不病，以其病病，是以不病。

Recognizing what one does not know is the highest order of behaviour
Pretending to knowledge one does not have is a fault of the worst kind
It is only by recognizing one's faults that one can be without fault
The enlightened man is without fault because he recognizes his faults
That is why he is without fault.

CHAPTER 72

Treasuring the Self

民不畏威，則大威至。無狎其所居，無厭其所生。夫唯不厭，是以不厭。是以聖人自知不自見；自愛不自貴。故去彼取此。

If the people are without awe
Something truly awful will happen to them
Do not violate their dwellings
Do not oppress their livelihood
If you do not oppress them
They will not respond in kind
The enlightened man knows himself without self-regard
Treasures himself but does not seek honour from others
He rejects the latter and acts on the former.

'Daoist immortal Li Tieguai receiving a visitor' (15th–16th centuries). Li was frequently depicted in popular culture; here, he addresses a formally dressed official who has come to pay respects.

'Outing to Zhang Gong's Grotto' – scroll painted by Zhu Ruoji (c. 1700).

The Net of the Dao

勇於敢則殺，勇於不敢則活。此兩者，或利或害。天之所惡，孰知其故？是以聖人猶難之。天之道，不爭而善勝，不言而善應，不召而自來，繟然而善謀。天網恢恢，疏而不失。

Courage to dare is fatal
Courage to dare not is salvation
There is benefit and harm in both of these
Who knows what Heaven abhors?
Even the enlightened man has trouble with this
The Dao is victorious without contending
Elicits response without speaking
Arrives without being summoned
Appears negligent but is carefully planned
The net of the Dao is vast and wide-meshed
But nothing escapes it.

CHAPTER 74

Accepting Responsibility

民不畏死，奈何以死懼之？若使民常畏死，而為奇者，吾得執而殺之，孰敢？常有司殺者殺。夫司殺者，是大匠斲；夫代大匠斲者，希有不傷其手矣。

If the people do not fear death
How can you scare them with the threat of death?
If they have a normal fear of death
When someone does something criminal
I arrest him and have him executed.
Who will then dare to repeat the offence?
Usually there is an official in charge of such matters who carries out the execution
If however someone stands in for that official
It is like someone trying to do the work of a master wood-worker
Few who try, escape uninjured.

'The Kangxi Emperor's Southern Inspection Tour', Scroll Three: Ji'nan to Mount Tai - handscroll by Wang Hui (1698).

In Daoism, 'Xian' describes an enlightened person, almost always immortal. They have, through self-reflection and devotion, reached a state of spiritual and physical immortality. Xian are often described as superhuman and with a variety of magical and supernatural abilities, such as immunity to heat and cold, the ability to fly and reach superhuman speeds. Some can survive on just air and dew, or can use their magic to bring death or grant life.

CHAPTER 75

Restraint

民之飢，以其上食稅之多，是以飢。民之難治，以其上之有為，是以難治。民之輕死，以其求生之厚，是以輕死。夫唯無以生為者，是賢於貴生。

If the people are starving

It is because the rulers tax their food too harshly

That is why the people starve

If the people are rebellious

It is because the government is too intrusive

That is why the people become rebellious

If the people don't take death seriously

It is because they are obsessed with the good things in life

That is why they don't take death seriously

It is those who do not strive after life

Who truly honour life.

CHAPTER 76

The Supple and Soft

人之生也柔弱，其死也堅強。萬物草木之生也柔脆，其死也枯槁。故堅強者死之徒，柔弱者生之徒。是以兵強則不勝，木強則折。強大處下，柔弱處上。

At birth man is supple and soft

At death he is firm and hard

In Creation plants and trees start out tender and fragile
But end up withered and rotten

Thus firmness and strength are the disciples of death

And suppleness and softness are those of life

If you rely on the strength of your army you will not be victorious

As a sturdy tree is ripe for felling

The great and strong come last

The supple and soft come first.

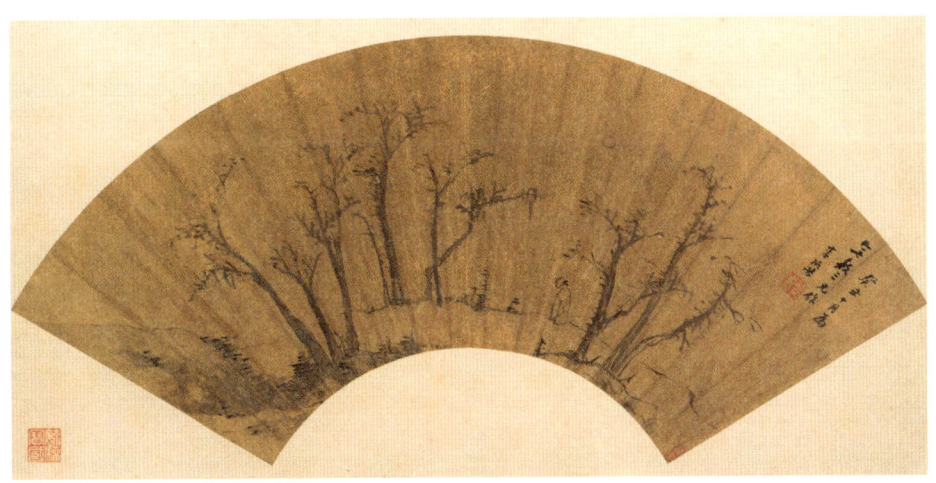

Using a folding fan as a base, artist Li Liufang used a few quickly-executed brushstrokes to sketch a stark vignette of a lone figure standing in a sparse grove of trees. The small circle above the figure's head is the moon; the shallow sense of space and the ghostly, pale ink may be attempts by the artist to capture the qualities of a moonlit landscape (1613).

CHAPTER 77

Like Drawing a Bow

天之道，其猶張弓與？高者抑之，下者舉之；有餘者損之，不足者補之。天之道，損有餘而補不足。人之道，則不然，損不足以奉有餘。孰能有餘以奉天下，唯有道者。是以聖人為而不恃，功成而不處，其不欲見賢。

Is not the Dao like the motion of drawing a bow?
The part that was low is raised up
And the part that was high is lowered
The excessive is decreased
The deficient augmented
The Dao decreases the excessive and augments the deficient
The way of man is otherwise
It further diminishes the deficient and augments the already excessive
Who is there who takes his own surplus and uses it to serve the world?
Only one who follows the Dao
Thus the enlightened man acts without expectation
Achieves without claiming credit
He has no desire to make a show of his virtue.

This full-length depiction of an imperial bodyguard of the first rank is from a set of one hundred portraits of loyal officials commissioned by the Qianlong emperor (r. 1736–95) that originally hung in the Hall of Imperial Brilliance, the pavilion in the Forbidden City, where the emperor received tribute offerings and entertained foreign emissaries.

CHAPTER 78

Straightforward but Paradoxical

天下莫柔弱於水，而攻堅強者莫之能勝，其無以易之。弱之勝強，柔之勝剛，天下莫不知，莫能行。是以聖人云：受國之垢，是謂社稷主；受國不祥，是謂天下王。正言若反。

There is nothing softer or more supple than water
Yet there is nothing better at overcoming the solid and strong
Nothing can substitute for it
The supple overcomes the solid
And the soft the strong

Everybody knows this
But none can put it into practice themselves
This is why the enlightened man says:
One who carries the guilt of the nation
May be called the lord of the ceremonial altars
One who carries the calamities of a nation
May be called ruler of the world
Straightforward words have paradoxical meanings.

CHAPTER 79

Impartiality

和大怨，必有餘怨；安可以為善？是以聖人執左契，而不責於人。有德司契，無德司徹。天道無親，常與善人。

When a great resentment is resolved
There is always a grudge left behind
How can this be a good thing?
For this reason the enlightened man may hold the creditor's half of the tally
But does not pursue the debt
A virtuous man considers the nature of the whole debt
A man without virtue sees only what benefits him
The Dao does not recognize partiality
So is always with the virtuous.

'Washing the Feet (from the Dusty World)', 1570. *A scholar on a boat in the middle ground bathes his feet in the cooling stream. The vast river scene is depicted from a high viewing point.*

CHAPTER 80

The Enlightened Ruler

小國寡民。使有什伯之器而不用；使民重死而不遠徙。雖有舟輿，無所乘之，雖有甲兵，無所陳之。使民復結繩而用之，甘其食，美其服，安其居，樂其俗。鄰國相望，雞犬之聲相聞，民至老死，不相往來。

An enlightened ruler, even if his state is small and population sparse,

May still make it so that his people will have no use for any number of new inventions

Will have no desire to flee even if they fear for their lives

Will have no desire to travel abroad even though they have boats and carriages

They may have fine armour and weapons, but will have no desire to display them

If the people return to the use of knotted cords to keep their records[11]

Their food will seem sweet to them

Their clothes beautiful

Their homes harmonious

And their way of life pleasing

Even if two neighbouring states are so close together

That they can hear each other's roosters and dogs

Even through old age and death

They will not feel the need for any contact.

---

[11] Before the development of the written numerical system, records and inventories were believed to have been kept using a system of knots in cords. There is no extant explanation of how this sytem might have worked in ancient China, but the reader might refer to the Inca system of "quipus".

CHAPTER 81

The Universal Dao

信言不美，美言不信。善者不辯，辯者不善。知者不博，博者不知。聖人不積，既以為人己愈有，既以與人己愈多。天之道，利而不害；聖人之道，為而不爭。

The truth is not beautiful
Fine words are not trustworthy
The good do not argue
The argumentative are not good
The wise do not try to know everything
Know-alls are not wise
The enlightened man is not acquisitive

But finds ample fulfilment in doing for others
And ample reward in giving to others
The universal Dao benefits without harming
The Dao of the enlightened man is to achieve without competing.

Laozi delivering a copy of the Tao Te Ching, *Ming dynasty, 17th century. Traditionally attributed to artist Li Gonglin.*

Index

Introduction	4
1. The Mystery of the Dao	9
2. Not-Doing	10
3. Removing Desire	13
4. The Infinite Dao	14
5. Cultivating Emptiness	16
6. The Spirit of the Valley	19
7. Self Through Selflessness	19
8. Avoiding Conflict	20
9. Recognizing Sufficiency	23
10. Potential of the Dao	24
11. The Power of the Insubstantial	27
12. Subjugation of Desire	28
13. Avoidance of Danger	30
14. The Essence of the Dao	31
15. Qualities of the Dao	33
16. Returning to Origin	34
17. The Natural Order	37
18. Neglecting the Dao	39
19. Diminishing the Self	40
20. Different from Others	42
21. The Origin of All Things	45
22. Restraint and Completion	46
23. Trust in the Dao	49
24. Left-over Food & Aimless Journeys	50
25. Natural Order	52
26. Gravity and Temperance	53
27. Deftness and Enlightenment	54
28. A River Valley to the World	57
29. Avoiding Extremes	58
30. Accordance with the Dao	61
31. The Sorrow of War	62
32. The Harmonious Dao	65
33. Longevity	66
34. The Pervasive Dao	69
35. The Inexhaustible Dao	71
36. Maintaining the Mystery of the Dao	72
37. Tranquillity	75
38. Avoidance of Chaos	76
39. Wisdom of the Ancients	79
40. Non-being	80
41. The Paradox of the Dao	82
42. The Basis of My Teaching	85
43. Achieved by Very Few	86
44. Ensuring Longevity	89
45. Order Under Heaven	91
46. At One With the Dao	92
47. Knowing Without Moving	94
48. Loss Upon Loss	95
49. The Enlightened Man	97
50. Life and Death	98
51. The Mysterious Process	101
52. Understanding the Infinite	102
53. The Winding By-ways	105
54. Cultivating Virtue	106
55. Purity of the New-Born	109
56. Honouring the Dao	110
57. Benefits of Simplicity	112
58. Sharp but Not Dangerous	114
59. Thrift	117
60. Doing No Harm	119
61. The Power of Receptiveness	121
62. Honouring the Dao	122
63. By Means of the Dao	124
64. Being Cautious	125
65. The Great Congruence of the Dao	129
66. Taking The Lower Position	130
67. Three Treasures	133
68. Following the Ancient Wisdom	134
69. Regretting Aggression	137
70. A Precious Jade	138
71. Recognizing One's Faults	141
72. Treasuring the Self	142
73. The Net of the Dao	145
74. Accepting Responsibility	146
75. Restraint	149
76. The Supple and Soft	150
77. Like Drawing a Bow	152
78. Straightforward but Paradoxical	154
79. Impartiality	155
80. The Enlightened Ruler	157
81. The Universal Dao	158